FASTING
AS UNTO THE
LORD

MARILYN SALMONSON

**WHITAKER
HOUSE**

The information presented here is not intended as medical advice. Always consult your physician before undertaking any change in your physical regimen, whether fasting, diet, or exercise.

FASTING AS UNTO THE LORD

ISBN: 0-88368-877-8
Printed in the United States of America
© 2000, 2003 by Marilyn Salmonson

Whitaker House
30 Hunt Valley Circle
New Kensington, PA 15068
web site: www.whitakerhouse.com

Library of Congress Cataloging-in-Publication Data

Salmonson, Marilyn, 1960–
 Fasting as unto the Lord / by Marilyn Salmonson.
  p. cm.
 ISBN 0-88368-877-8 (alk. paper)
 1. Fasting. I. Title.
BV5055.S35 2003
248.4'7—dc21

                                    2002154456

 1 2 3 4 5 6 7 8 9 10 11 12 13 / 12 11 10 09 08 07 06 05 04 03

Contents

———◦◦⟨∞⟩◦◦———

Foreword

*F*asting is more than denying oneself food; it is a way of life. Isaiah 58 explains what a *true* fast is. It is not just a day to humble oneself before God. Along with denying ourselves food and living a life of humility before God, we must also be servants to our brothers and sisters.

Isaiah 58 also tells us what a fasting lifestyle will do for us. Fasting brings humility, loosens the chains of injustice, unties the cords of the yoke, sets the oppressed free, feeds the hungry, provides for the poor, and clothes the naked. This cannot be done in just a matter of days. It must be a commitment of oneself and an act of servitude to God.

God tells us in Isaiah what will happen as we develop a fasting lifestyle:

> *Then your light will break forth like the dawn, and your healing will quickly appear; then your righteousness will go before you, and the glory of the LORD will be your rear guard. Then you will call, and the LORD will answer; you will cry for help, and he will say: Here am I.*
> (Isaiah 58:8–9 NIV)

The last part of Isaiah 58:12 says it all. God says we will be called *"Repairer[s] of Broken Walls, Restorer[s] of Streets with Dwellings."* Praise God!

Fasting has become like a spiritual mirror for me. It forces me to look at myself through God's eyes, and it reveals the truth of my spiritual walk with Him. I believe fasting reflects the soul and brings forth the spiritual man so that God can properly align the temple—spirit, soul, and *then* the body.

In *Fasting as unto the Lord*, Marilyn Salmonson truly reflects what fasting is all about. In reading this book, you will hear the Spirit of God speaking through Marilyn. She has used sound wisdom, detailed knowledge, and godly counsel from Christian professionals who have spent years researching the benefits of fasting. I highly recommend this book to anyone who wants a closer daily walk with the Lord Jesus Christ.

—Lloyd Bustard
International speaker, music artist,
prophet, and pastor of
World Worship Center, N.C.

Prologue

I would like to take a moment to share with you the small miracle of how this book came to be. God always has a plan for our lives, even if we do not know what it is at times. Stay focused on the Word of God, and He will birth concepts, ideas, and visions in you that you have never imagined nor thought you could ever possess.

This book was inspired during a year and six months of my own partial fasting as unto the Lord. At the beginning of each year, the Lord has always given me a word to encourage and strengthen my walk for the year. In 1997, His words to my spirit were "prepare in prayer." And so I began praying more often and for longer periods of time.

That year proved to be one of strengthening my prayer life. I witnessed tremendous victories in my life and in the lives of my family members because of the seeds of prayer I sowed during that time. Now, as a result, my prayer life has been multiplied bountifully.

In 1998, the Lord revealed three words to my spirit during prayer—"fasting," "no compromise," and "repentance," in that order. Well, I immediately incorporated fasting into my walk, and this book is the fruit of my labor.

I share this wonderful information from the Word of God, and I pray it will serve you as it did me. The result has proven to be an equipping of my spirit man, which has propelled me to the next level in my Christian walk.

I have taken another step upward toward the center of God's will for my life, and this has given me a deeper appreciation for the ways, the will, and the Word of God.

—Marilyn Salmonson

Chapter One

---•◦⟨∞⟩◦•---

The Benefits of Fasting

1

The Benefits of Fasting

G od has selected fasting as a tool for believers. It is a tool meant to loose the bands of wickedness—a tool with the purpose of setting believers free from the enemy so that they can live lives of victory.

Is this not the fast that I have chosen: to loose the bonds of wickedness, to undo the heavy burdens, to let the oppressed go free, and that you break every yoke?
(Isaiah 58:6)

But how does fasting accomplish this?

Fasting Empowers Your Spirit Man

Through the separation of spirit and body achieved through fasting, the spirit man is given freedom to rule over the mortal body.

When and how does this occur? It occurs at the moment during the fast when your natural man surrenders control to your spirit man. As this takes place, the flesh is simultaneously crucified, and you then depend only on the Holy Spirit to sustain you.

The brief moment of separation between your spirit and your physical nature is what propels you forward in your Christian walk. Using moments like these, God continues to change you, more and more, into His own image.

> *But we all, with unveiled face, beholding as in a mirror the glory of the Lord, are being transformed into the same image from glory to glory, just as by the Spirit of the Lord.*   (2 Corinthians 3:18)

Being transformed into God's image means being transformed into a person of holiness, righteousness, compassion, and love. However, He can only accomplish this transformation if you surrender your will to His perfect will, and your spirit to His Holy Spirit.

How do you surrender your will to His will? Through true repentance and by not compromising the Word of God in your life through submission to the seductions of this world, which are contrary to the truths of the Holy Scriptures. Be a doer of the Word and not just a hearer of it, for His Word commands it!

> *But be doers of the word, and not hearers only, deceiving yourselves.* (James 1:22)

The process of surrendering your will to His and allowing Him to govern your life is activated more readily and abundantly through prayer, praise, worship, and fasting.

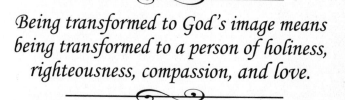

Being transformed to God's image means being transformed to a person of holiness, righteousness, compassion, and love.

When you pray, you are in communication with God, realizing His will for your life because He reveals it to you. Praise helps you to experience His joy; fasting strengthens your spirit and causes His will to be manifested in your life.

A Spirit Man Empowered

I asked brother Richard H. Meisel, a wonderful man of God and the president and associate pastor of Hall Deliverance Foundation, Inc., to share an experience he had with fasting when he was still a new believer. This is what he had to say about his time of spiritual growth.

In the summer of 1980, I was playing keyboard for a country western band in Springerville, Arizona. Earlier in the year, I had started getting hives all over my body. My doctor said I was most likely allergic to something, so I tried getting rid of my cat, changing clothes, using different soap, etc., to no avail. I was told that it would cost one thousand dollars to do blood tests, and even then they might not know exactly what was causing the allergic reaction.

My doctor gave me a prescription with strong antihistamine medicine in it. It brought relief, but it also made me feel a lot different: I started to periodically lose feeling in an arm or a leg, similar to when an extremity "falls asleep." It was awful and a little scary.

At that time, I was reading a book entitled *Because of Your Unbelief,* written by the Reverend Franklin Hall, given to me by a friend. I believed what Hall said about fasting; it agreed with what I had often thought about the subject. Back in Pennsylvania, where I was born, I would read articles in the paper about miners trapped underground. I took notice, as I read, that when they were without food for the period of their entrapment, they recorded seeing heavenly visions (which the world would call hallucinations). I also was aware that people adrift at sea without food would often see the Lord, or angels, etc. So I had surmised that fasting was spiritual. Although I wanted to fast, I was ignorant about the process of fasting and thought I wouldn't be able to fast and work at the same time.

However, reading Franklin Hall's book started to give me faith that I could participate in a fast to receive healing from my allergic reaction, thereby getting rid of the medicine and its bad side effects. I believed that my body would live on and consume the toxins in my body, making me feel better. I also believed that fasting would make my words, spoken in prayer, have more power when I communed with the Father.

I fasted, drinking only water, for twenty days. I was healed on about the fourteenth day from the ailments that had plagued me. I also grew spiritually. I experienced an urgency to know Jesus in a more intimate way, and I gained discernment. God spoke audibly to me on the twentieth day and said three times consecutively, "Tell Me." I discerned that He wanted me to communicate my desires and petitions through prayer, and so I did. Praise our Lord Jesus Christ!

After the fast, I wanted to meet the man who wrote the book that had so influenced me, so I visited the church that he and his wife, the Reverends Franklin and Helen Hall, shepherded: the International Healing Cathedral.

I can attribute the positive changes in my life to God, Jesus, the Holy Spirit, and fasting. I quit the band I had been in and became a part of Reverend Franklin Hall's church; I have continued there for over twenty-two years. Thank You, Jesus!

Fasting is a must. It not only cleanses the body, but it makes our spiritual lives better.

"When the Bridegroom is taken away, then shall they fast." (See Mark 2:20.) Jesus said this when asked by the

Pharisees why He and His disciples were not fasting, especially when John the Baptist and his disciples did. In a sense, we should fast because our Savior, our Bridegroom, is in heaven. We have a reason to fast until He returns. Let's all fast, pray, and put on Christ, coming into the unity of the faith!

Fasting Enhances Your Prayer Life

Fasting enhances your prayer life by strengthening your desire to commune with the Father in prayer throughout each day. There is an alertness, an awareness, that occurs in your spirit on a daily basis. Through fasting, you gain the ears to hear His prompting as He addresses you in each situation.

Fasting enhances your prayer life by strengthening your desire to commune with the Father.

Your acknowledgment, through prayer, of the presence of God in your everyday life will cause you to similarly acknowledge the benefits provided to you as a result of His presence. These benefits take many forms. They include:

1. Favor

2. Divine appointments

3. Protection

4. Wisdom

5. Knowledge

6. Understanding

7. Discernment

8. Revelation

9. Concepts

10. Strategies and ideas

These benefits will be visible to you during and after a fast because you will be seeing with the eyes of your spirit, enlightened by the Holy Spirit—a direct result of your fast. Fasting will always strengthen your spirit and cause you to see and experience the benefits of the spiritual realm, even here in the physical realm. (Remember, the natural laws are always subject to the spiritual laws.) All of a sudden, you will be making withdrawals from God's reserve of spiritual benefits because of your increased faith in Him, which is the key needed to make the withdrawal.

Although these benefits have always been there for you to draw from in any given situation, it is because of your fast that you realize their existence and begin to use them in your daily decision-making. God bestows all of these benefits upon you as a way of causing victory in your life.

In 1 Thessalonians 5:17, the Word commands, *"Pray without ceasing."* Why? Because, as you commune with the Father and as your prayers are released in the physical realm, there are many benefits that await you. Your prayers open opportunities for the spiritual realm to manifest change in the physical world you live in.

Christians often believe that they are supposed to chase after God's attention. Yet He already gives us His full concentration, desiring our attention, just as we desire His. It is He who prompts us to commune with Him in prayer throughout the day, so that He can be instrumental in our daily victories.

Keep in mind that, ultimately, the victories we achieve in our lives happen because of God's intervention. Without His intervention, we would have few victories or none at all, according to the dimensions of what He desires us to achieve. In other words, what we call victory by our own efforts could never compare to the triumph He could have caused had we allowed His prompting, delivered by His Holy Spirit, to handle the situation differently. Instead, we put the cart before the horse by not submitting to prayer and by not waiting on His answer to the problem.

His prompting is for the purpose of moving us to acknowledge our dependence on Him—to show us that it is His intervention in our lives that causes us to bring Him glory in all we do. It is when we seek Him that He seeks us. It is when we seek Him that we express, confirm, and validate His position in our lives.

Franklin Hall, the author of the book *Atomic Power with God with Fasting and Prayer,* helps to identify another powerful point that describes how fasting enhances your prayer life. He makes an important distinction between two forms of prayer:

1. Prayer

2. Fasting prayer

The first form of prayer refers to prayer expressed without the aid of fasting. Blessing a meal before you eat would be an example of this form of prayer.

The second form of prayer refers to "prayer prayed under the influence of fasting."[1] Fasting

---

[1] Reverend F. Hall, *Atomic Power with God with Fasting and Prayer,* page 7.

prayers are tools used to transform prayers of unbelief to faith. "Fasting restores and amplifies prayer power."[2]

A Testimony of Fasting Prayer

I asked Bernadette Clayborne, a dear sister in the Lord, to share the testimony of her son's victory, which took place with the added ammunition of fasting in her life. This is what she had to share:

> I recall one morning I was at the end of my rope. Something was very wrong with my son, and I couldn't help him. Kyle was in kindergarten, and it was becoming more and more difficult to leave him at his classroom door. He would cry, foam at the mouth, grind his teeth, and scream loudly. It would disturb the entire class; some of the other children would start to look a little sad, and sometimes they would even start to cry themselves.
>
> That morning he had such a terrible fit that it took two teachers to hold him. Kyle's teachers told me to leave, saying that he would calm down. So I left the

---

[2] Ibid., page 7.

school while my son was still screaming, "Mommy, help me. Don't leave me!" My heart was broken. This was my baby, and I couldn't help him.

Exiting the school, I was visibly shaken and in tears. I had had it with these fits! I poured my heart out to God about my son during the car ride home. He was so young and helpless; I wanted whatever was wrong to be fixed. I prayed: "Please, Lord, reveal to me what is wrong with my child so that I can help him."

It is when we seek Him that He seeks us.

That morning, feeling compassion and concern for Kyle, sister Marilyn stopped by his classroom. She and the class teacher laid hands on Kyle and began praying for him. He did calm down a little and had a peaceful day. Marilyn phoned me at home later that morning and told me what had taken place. She told me that, as she was praying, the Lord had revealed that Kyle could not hear well. She said, "I see in the Spirit that there is something wrong with his hearing." I told her that he had passed a hearing test earlier but that I would take him to the doctor to get another test.

I took Kyle to the doctor the next day and told the doctor about the problems Kyle was experiencing at school. I also told him about Marilyn's spiritual revelation concerning Kyle's hearing. He gave Kyle another hearing test to put my mind at ease and, through our conversation, I learned that the doctor and his family were also Christians.

The test results came back normal. However, I knew that God had spoken to Marilyn, and I was determined to get to the root of Kyle's problem. He was my baby; it hurt me to see him in such distress. I decided to go on a fast for three days. No food, just water until 6:00 p.m. After six o'clock, I would have a light dinner and no dessert. During the fast, I got up early in the morning to read my Bible, sing, and pray. While driving in the car, I played gospel music and talked to God some more.

A few months before, I had bought a ministry tape on spiritual warfare. I decided to listen to it one more time just to see if there was anything new for me to learn. On the third day of my fast, I listened to the tape and realized that the enemies of my soul are strongholds. I needed to stop wasting time binding little spirits and start binding the strongholds instead. The tape helped me understand that this was the way to bind the power of Satan.

As the tape continued, the speaker began to tell the story of the boy with the *"dumb and deaf spirit"* that the disciples could not drive out.

25 He rebuked the unclean spirit, saying to it, "Deaf and dumb spirit, I command you, come out of him and enter him no more!"

26 Then the spirit cried out, convulsed him greatly, and came out of him. And he became as one dead, so that many said, "He is dead."

27 But Jesus took him by the hand and lifted him up, and he arose.

28 And when He had come into the house, His disciples asked Him privately, "Why could we not cast it out?"

29 So He said to them, "This kind can come out by nothing but prayer and fasting." (Mark 9:25–29)

I knew immediately what was wrong with Kyle. He had experienced all the same symptoms as the boy in the story. The Holy Spirit revealed to me what needed to be done. (Thank You, Holy Spirit, for loving Kyle and me so much!)

Later that evening, and on the drive to school the next day, I prayed for my son and rebuked Satan: "Satan, Kyle belongs to the Lord. You are trespassing on blood bought property. I rebuke you, dumb and deaf stronghold spirit. No longer can you block Kyle's spiritual hearing and receiving from God. Your powers over Kyle's life are destroyed; do not return again, in the name of Jesus!" That morning, I left Kyle at his classroom with a smile on his face. He was a changed person and has been delivered from the deaf and dumb spirit ever since. Praise God!

Bernadette's testimony of Kyle's victory is an example of the power released when prayer is combined with fasting.

Together, prayer and fasting will help to still your mind and to focus your thoughts so that you can hear God's voice. Pray and fast! The two go hand in hand!

Fasting Helps You Focus on Your Christian Walk

The result of staying focused in your Christian walk is a harvest of blessings in your life and in the lives of the people you are interceding for in prayer. Why? The answer is simple. When you are called to fast and you are obedient to God's call, God will honor you and your prayers.

Fasting is an exercise that empowers your spirit. It makes your spirit man stronger, and your flesh weaker. As a result, we are more readily able to surrender to the Holy Spirit.

I say then: Walk in the Spirit, and you shall not fulfill the lust of the flesh.
(Galatians 5:16)

The surrender of your will to His perfect will allows you to maintain your Christian walk. Fasting helps you to stay focused on the path toward God's ordained destiny for your life.

Never forget that God knows your weaknesses. He will put in your heart a desire to fast so that you will be prepared to overcome specific situations in your life. Why does He do this? Because He loves you and wants to bless you—always!

Varying Benefits of Fasting

I would like to note that the benefits of fasting may vary according to three areas of growth in your walk with Jesus Christ:

1. Faith Level

2. Commitment Level

3. Application of the Word

Faith Level

When it comes to the degree of benefits experienced from your fast, the amount of time you have been a Christian will prove to make a difference. The Christian who has been a believer for many years will, at times, have a greater faith level than the new Christian, who has not yet experienced the exercising of faith in his or her life.

Never forget that God knows your weaknesses.

A good example of the differences between experienced faith and inexperienced faith is found in the account of the prophet Elisha and his servant. For it is Elisha who saw clearly into the spiritual realm and was able to see the angels surrounding them in battle to protect and aid them in their victory against the Syrians.

> *15 And when the servant* [Elisha] *arose early and went out, there was an army, surrounding the city with horses and chariots. And his servant said to him, "Alas, my master! What shall we do?"*

> *16 So he answered, "Do not fear, for those who are with us are more than those who are with them."*

> *17 And Elisha prayed, and said, "LORD, I pray, open his eyes that he may see." Then the LORD opened the eyes of the young man, and he saw. And behold, the mountain was full of horses and chariots of fire all around Elisha.*

(2 Kings 6:15–17)

Faith is explained in chapter eleven of the book of Hebrews as, *"the substance of things hoped for, the evidence of things not seen"* (verse 1). To experience the greater things of God is to catch a glimpse of what is in the spiritual realm through the exercising of your faith.

If you have been at a place where your faith has been challenged, you have experienced a deeper exercising of faith. If you are a seasoned

Christian, then you have experienced a greater level of faith. You have had more time to condition and exercise your faith. Faith grows when it is challenged.

> *13 For everyone who partakes only of milk is unskilled in the word of righteousness, for he is a babe.*
>
> *14 But solid food belongs to those who are of full age, that is, those who by reason of use have their senses exercised to discern both good and evil.*
>
> (Hebrews 5:13–14)

Commitment Level

Commitment level refers to the time you spend pursuing the things of God through prayer (your mode of communication with God), praise (singing of His blessings), worship (revering Him), and fasting (crucifying your flesh as He crucified His). These pursuits of God will lead you to a greater acknowledgment of His presence and to a deeper relationship with the Holy Spirit.

The greater the commitment level, the greater the faith level, and vice versa. A greater faith level produces greater experiences in the things of God—particularly in prayer, praise, worship, and fasting, which are elements of commitment. Similarly, a greater commitment level produces a greater faith level because, through the elements of commitment, you acknowledge God's presence and fulfilled promises in your life, building your faith.

Application of the Word

The application of the Word means making the Word of God effective in your life. In order to make the Word of God active in your life, you must learn to apply it to every situation in your life. To do that, follow these three steps:

1. Identify the area in your life that needs to change.

2. Find Scripture that deals with that specific situation and make it yours by inserting your name. An example is: ~~Ann Seemer~~ (your name) is a wise man (or woman) who cautiously avoids evil." (See Proverbs 14:16 NAS.)

3. Confess the Scripture (with your name) over yourself and/or your situation, and you will see results!

So shall My word be that goes forth out of My mouth: it shall not return to Me void [without producing any effect, useless], but

*it shall accomplish that which I please and
purpose, and it shall prosper in the thing
for which I sent it.* (Isaiah 55:11 AMP)

Apply the Word of God to your life. Activate it
by confessing it! Your confessions will ignite your
faith. They will light a match in the middle of
your dark area or situation so that you can see
the answer clearly. Through the application of
the Word in your life, God will reveal His wisdom
in the what, when, where, and how of handling
any given situation.

Knowledge alone is not enough to bring the
victories God desires for you to have. Therefore,
experience the effectiveness of His Word by seek-
ing God with all of your mind, your soul, and
your might, and you will become more "in tune"
with the will of God for your life.

Chapter Two

Staying on the Path

2

Staying on the Path

———•·❧❧·•———

I have prepared several illustrations to show how your commitment level and faith level, discussed in chapter one, affect your Christian walk. These diagrams should help you understand how fasting can help you reach the center of God's will.

Diagram A (page 43) shows a hypothetical Christian at one hundred percent commitment to his or her Christian walk.

In this diagram, the circle represents the center of God's will for our lives. The shaded triangular area represents the path (our Christian walk) to the center of God's will. We must stay on the path.

Our objective, as Christians, should be to find the center of God's will for our lives. Why? Because it is only when we arrive at the center of God's will that we can effectively fulfill all that He has for us to accomplish for the kingdom and for His glory.

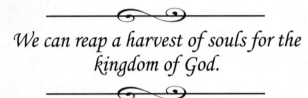

We can reap a harvest of souls for the kingdom of God.

Walking on the path of one hundred percent commitment, we reach the center of God's will for our lives the quickest (provided that we make no deviations from the path). This direct path allows Christians to spend the least amount of time in unproductive behavior that doesn't profit the kingdom of God.

By being in the center of God's will, we accomplish His will for our lives and the lives of others. We can help them, using the manifestation of God in our lives. We can reap a harvest of souls for the kingdom of God.

Thus, we take hold of all the promises of God made available to us as believers. As His children, we are entitled to partake of them.

Here are some examples of those promises:

1. We have eternal life.

Because if you acknowledge and confess with your lips that Jesus is Lord and in your heart believe (adhere to, trust in, and rely on the truth) that God raised Him from the dead, you will be saved.
(Romans 10:9 AMP)

2. He will never leave us.

Be strong and of good courage, do not fear nor be afraid of them; for the Lord your God, He is the One who goes with you. He will not leave you nor forsake you. (Deuteronomy 31:6)

3. We will have peace.

I will listen to what God the LORD will say; he promises peace to his people, his saints. (Psalm 85:8 NIV)

We have been given great and precious promises. Take ownership of them, and watch them come to fruition in your life by staying focused and committed to Him.

Through these he has given us his very great and precious promises, so that through them you may participate in

*the divine nature and escape the corrup-
tion in the world caused by evil desires.*
(2 Peter 1:4 NIV)

Hypothetically, most Christians' relationships with God are not even near the sixty percent commitment level. Therefore, it is very difficult for them to take hold of all God's promises and experience those promises operating in their lives, which would cause them to be victorious in every area of their Christian walk. They struggle every day with greater shortcomings in their journey toward God's will.

We have been given great and precious promises. Take ownership of them and watch them come to fruition in your life.

Our goal as Christians should be to increase the level of commitment in our Christian walk and to grow every day in the things of God, thus allowing God to convert our weaknesses into strengths so that we can live victorious lives here on earth through the proper application of the Word in our daily lives.

TO GET TO THE CENTER OF THE CIRCLE, STAY ON THE PATH

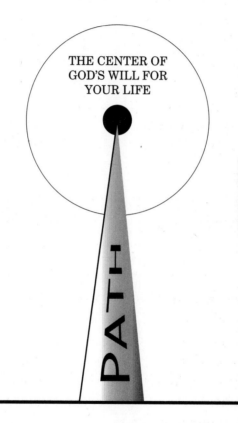

THE CENTER OF GOD'S WILL FOR YOUR LIFE

PATH

A CHRISTIAN AT 100% COMMITMENT IN HIS/HER CHRISTIAN WALK

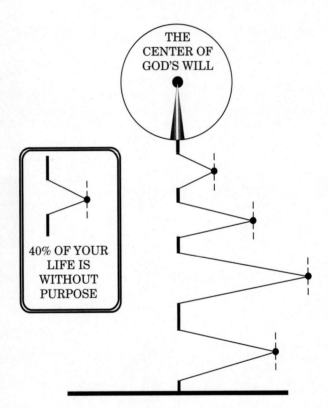

THE
CENTER OF
GOD'S WILL

40% OF YOUR
LIFE IS
WITHOUT
PURPOSE

A CHRISTIAN WALK AT APPROXIMATELY
60% COMMITMENT LEVEL

DIAGRAM C

YOUR GOAL AS A CHRISTIAN

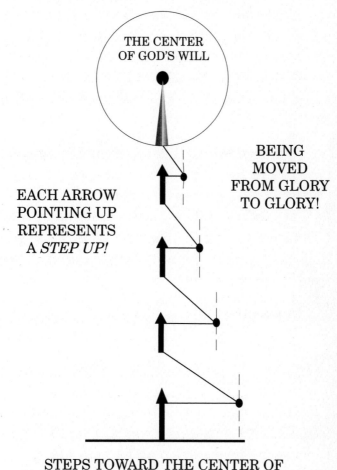

THE CENTER
OF GOD'S WILL

EACH ARROW
POINTING UP
REPRESENTS
A *STEP UP!*

BEING
MOVED
FROM GLORY
TO GLORY!

STEPS TOWARD THE CENTER OF
GOD'S WILL FOR YOUR LIFE

Diagram B (page 44) shows an example of a Christian at a sixty percent commitment level. In this diagram, the circle represents the center of God's will for our lives. The line represents the Christian walk. The lines leading to the points off the path represent time spent distracted from the path. These distractions often take the form of obstacles, which cause us to lose speed on our way to the center of God's will for our lives.

The objective of this diagram is to put into perspective the amount of time spent in unproductive behavior versus the amount of time spent in God's service. When you are only sixty percent committed to God in your Christian walk, what happens to the remaining forty percent of your time? How is it spent?

In temptation?

In sin?

In confusion?

The correct answer is all of the above. The leftover forty percent is a waste of your time, lost because of the enemy's plan for your life.

Yes, the enemy has a plan for you! The devil wants to destroy all that God has for you. He does not want you to reach your goal as a Christian. If the devil succeeds, you will not be able to partake of God's promises and His blessings for your life. If you are led away by Satan's distractions, you cannot fulfill the purpose and destiny that God has ordained for your life.

> *Before I formed you in the womb I knew you; Before you were born I sanctified you; I ordained you a prophet to the nations.* (Jeremiah 1:5)

Diagram C (page 45) shows arrows pointed upward toward the center of God's will. These arrows represent stages, or victory steps, taken after overcoming the distractions (obstacles) that had previously caused straying from the path.

The lines leading to the points off the path represent time spent on distractions (unproductive behavior).

⟡Note: As you continue to climb the steps of victory over obstacles shown on the graph, the time you spend off the path decreases. This represents the growth in your Christian walk, being moved from glory to glory, toward the center of God's will for your life.

How do we allow God to help us in our quest to reach the center of His will for our lives? We allow Him to change us and take us to the next level (from glory to glory) when we use the tools He has given us in His Word to overcome the obstacles in our lives.

The Tools

God has given us His Word with the purpose of instructing us in the use of His tools. These tools strengthen us so that we can be victorious in all things and overcome the enemy.

> *But thanks be to God, Who gives us the victory [making us conquerors] through our Lord Jesus Christ.*
> (1 Corinthians 15:57 AMP)

We are also given the tools for the fulfilling of God's purpose and destiny in our lives.

> *For I know the thoughts that I think toward you, saith the LORD, thoughts of peace, and not of evil, to give you an expected end.* (Jeremiah 29:11 KJV)

What Are the Tools?

1. Repentance: Confessing our sin and getting right with God.

2. Prayer: Communication with the Father.

3. Praise and Worship: Ways to honor the Lord, remind us of His victories, and restore our joy.

4. Fasting: The exercise and conditioning of the spirit.

These tools, when applied to our lives, help us to narrow the space of time spent offtrack. Remember, the more we can reduce the amount of time spent offtrack, the faster we can reach the center of God's will.

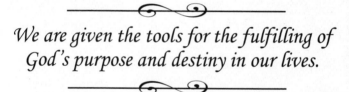

We are given the tools for the fulfilling of God's purpose and destiny in our lives.

Using these tools will help us to achieve our goal and reach the center of God's will. There, we can fulfill the purpose and destiny God has for us by being effective for the glory of the kingdom of God.

The Armor

God has also provided His protection for us as we use His tools and strive to follow His will.

Then shall your light shall break forth like the morning, and your healing (your restoration and the power of a new life)

shall spring forth speedily; your righteous-
ness (your rightness, your justice, and
your right relationship with God) shall go
before you [conducting you to peace and
prosperity], and the glory of the Lord shall
be your rear guard.   (Isaiah 58:8 AMP)

In this verse, the Lord has revealed a wonderful example of how His protection is bestowed upon us to bring us to victory.

The phrase *"rear guard"* describes a body of troops who are detached from the main force to protect the rear.[1]

The rear guard, as God revealed it to me, represents abiding under the shadow of the Almighty.

He who dwells in the secret place of the
Most High Shall abide under the shadow
of the Almighty.   (Psalm 91:1)

Another example of God's protection is found in Ephesians.

[13] *Therefore take up the whole armor of*
God, that you may be able to withstand in
the evil day, and having done all, to stand.

---

[1] *The Merriam-Webster New Collegiate Dictionary,*
page 955.

14 Stand therefore, having girded your waist with truth, having put on the breastplate of righteousness,

15 and having shod your feet with the preparation of the gospel of peace;

16 above all, taking the shield of faith with which you will be able to quench all the fiery darts of the wicked one.

17 And take the helmet of salvation, and the sword of the Spirit, which is the word of God. (Ephesians 6:13–17)

God has given us the:

Helmet of Salvation

Breastplate of Righteousness

Gospel of Truth

Preparation of the Gospel of Peace

Shield of Faith

Sword of the Spirit (God's Word)

All of these items protect us from the front while God's own shadow, His rear guard, protects us from the back. To have the Lord cover you with His shadow is to be protected completely from the enemy. What a wonderful God we serve!

God wants us to have victory in all areas, and He has given us the tools we need to succeed. Fasting is one of the tools. Learn to use the tools by studying the Bible, God's Word!

Testimony of the Tool of Fasting

I asked Pastor Singletary, who has been in the ministry for over twenty years, to explain how the benefits of fasting have strengthened his Christian walk. He candidly shared his system, which helped him to address each area of opportunity in his life and bring him to the center of God's will for his life.

As a child, I had a love for the things of God and the church. I loved pretending to be the pastor or that praying deacon who made it seem as if heaven had come down to earth. I can remember reenacting church services while playing with friends on some Sunday afternoons. As I grew older, there was nothing more exciting to me than the idea of becoming a pastor.

Maturing into adulthood, I realized that there was nothing I wanted to do more than to serve God. As time passed, I felt in my heart that I'd been called to preach the Gospel. My pastor confirmed what was in my heart.

I knew that I wasn't just a preacher, but a pastor. God not only gifted me with the ability to preach, but He also gifted me in music ministry. I played the keyboard, directed choirs, and led praise and worship. I became very visible in this area of ministry. For this reason, people had the tendency to see me as a minister of music rather than a pastor. Since things were going so well for me in music ministry, I became comfortable and didn't want to stretch myself. Settled, but not satisfied, my desire was to be a pastor, and there was only one way for me to get out of my comfort zone.

I'm not one for moving fast when it comes to decisions about the things of God. I have to know that I'm doing the right thing before I act. Fasting, for me, was the only one sure way of knowing God's will—and the one sure way of getting out of my comfort zone.

I entered a fast of five days, using the following system made available to me by God. He had me take five index cards and number them according to the number of days in the fast. On each card, I wrote the area of focus where

I felt the Holy Spirit leading me to improve. During each day of the fast, God and I communed in prayer so He could reveal His insight and give the answers I desired for the fulfillment of my purpose and destiny. Each day, I focused on the specific area addressed on that day's card. I prayed about nothing else.

My prayer cards read as follows:

Day 1: Relationship—
Draw nearer to God and secure His presence for a lifetime of intimacy with Him.

Day 2: Ministry—
Examine my call to pastor and to plant a church; am I ready?

Day 3: Mentoring—
Reveal my earthly mentor.

Day 4: Warfare—
Expose roots of bitterness, anger, and malice that may exist in any given area of my life and/or those who surround me.

Day 5: Things—
Petition God for personal things.

God honored this time of fasting and prayer. Today I am pastoring a great group of people in South Florida. God is faithful!

Let's be movers and shakers for the kingdom of God! Let's follow the apostle Paul's footsteps as recorded in 1 Corinthians 2:1–5.

¹ And I, brethren, when I came to you, did not come with excellence of speech or of wisdom declaring to you the testimony of God.

² For I determined not to know anything among you except Jesus Christ and Him crucified.

³ I was with you in weakness, in fear, and in much trembling.

⁴ And my speech and my preaching were not with persuasive words of human wisdom, but in demonstration of the Spirit and of power,

⁵ that your faith should not be in the wisdom of men but in the power of God.

Paul preached with power and demonstration. Let's do the greater works that

Jesus said we could do! Let's accomplish it all. How? Through fasting and prayer!

Fasting Is the Key

Fasting is the key to understanding what God's purpose and destiny is for your life. It is a tool to help you stay on the path of full commitment that leads to the center of God's will.

Drs. Ken and Mary Jane Brewer, along with their son Christopher, have established Brewer Christian College and Graduate Schools, an extensive Internet school, dedicated to training and establishing ministers in the service of the kingdom of God. As a family, they have grown to know and understand the importance of prayer and fasting in determining God's will. Mary Jane Brewer shared their testimony:

> Over two decades ago, Ken and I found ourselves at a great crossroads. Living in an affluent suburb of Chicago with our two young sons, Ken's business career looked bright. As a young man, he had already received great recognition in the business world and now, working for a large medical lab supply company, he was quickly climbing his way up the corporate ladder. But Ken and I found ourselves empty and disillusioned with the

direction our lives had taken. We both sensed the Lord was calling us to surrender our future to full-time service for our Lord and Savior Jesus Christ.

In this crucial hour of decision, we chose to devote our lives to fasting and praying until we received a clear answer from the Lord. After two weeks, the Lord brought the answer in a simple phone call. An evangelist we had recently met, who was not aware of what was going on in our lives, felt led to call and tell us about a church in a small town in Ohio that was looking for a pastor. Even though we had never pastored, and Ken had never preached to more than a handful of people in his life, we knew that this was indeed the Lord's answer to our prayers. We needed to go.

We are still amazed when we look back at this event, which launched us on an amazing new journey of faith. Because of that time of concerted effort in prayer and fasting, we were led into full-time ministry. We witnessed the transformation of many lives as result of our answered call to serve the Lord. We went on to pastor several churches, a few of which we pioneered on our own, and continued to witness the hand of the Lord continually bringing answer after answer during times committed to concentrated prayer and fasting.

God's plan for our lives has been, and always will be, to transpose us from one level of growth to the next. He desires a constant improvement over what already exists in our spirit and in our intellect. It is the divine wisdom we acquire from every obstacle we overcome by Christ Jesus that brings this improvement in spirit. And fasting equips us to overcome those obstacles.

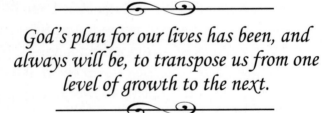

God's plan for our lives has been, and always will be, to transpose us from one level of growth to the next.

How quickly you move to the center of God's will has to do with how readily you surrender your natural man to your spirit man. The more you fast, the more you will become aware of the spirit man in your life. This will allow you to walk the path to God's will with greater confidence.

And after holding to the correct path, using the tools and protection God has provided, you may say, like Job,

[11] *My foot has held fast to His steps; I have kept His way and not turned aside.*

[12] *I have not departed from the commandment of His lips; I have treasured the words of His mouth more than my necessary food.* (Job 23:11–12)

Chapter Three

What Is a Fast?

3

What Is a Fast?

─────•·◦∞◦·•─────

asting is the discipline of abstaining
from food or drink for spiritual purposes.
The Bible speaks of four types of fasts.

The Partial Fast

In this type of fast, at least one of the following is abstained from: one meal a day; one meal
a week; or pleasant foods, such as dessert.

The earliest example of a fast to honor God is
located in the first book of the Bible.

> ¹⁶ *And the* LORD *God commanded the man, saying, "Of every tree of the garden you may freely eat;*
>
> ¹⁷ *"but of the tree of the knowledge of good and evil you shall not eat, for in the day that you eat of it you shall surely die."* (Genesis 2:16–17)

In a sense, this command from God was for the first fast—a partial fast, in which one specific food is abstained from. In this case, the prohibited food was the fruit from the Tree of Knowledge of Good and Evil.

The intention of this partial fast was to strengthen man against the wickedness of the enemy.

This fast was to serve Adam and Eve by:

1. Giving them strength to overcome the enemy.

2. Giving them discipline for their lives.

3. Helping them to show respect or reverence for God.

4. Reminding them that God desires obedience to His commands.

The same is true today! Our fasts, while they serve God, also serve us in each of these four ways.

The book of Daniel shows us another example of a partial fast when Daniel denied himself enjoyable food during a three-week period of mourning.

> *I ate no pleasant food, no meat or wine came into my mouth, nor did I anoint myself at all, till three whole weeks were fulfilled.* (Daniel 10:3)

The Absolute Fast

In this type of fast, all solid foods and liquids, including water, are abstained from. (This kind of fast should not be practiced for more than three days because your body will start to dehydrate.)

In the book of Acts, Saul underwent an absolute fast after he was converted on the road to Damascus. A light from the heavens blinded Saul as Jesus spoke to him on the road. He remained blind for three days and did not eat or drink during that time.

> *8 Then Saul arose from the ground, and when his eyes were opened he saw no one. But they led him by the hand and brought him into Damascus.*
>
> *9 And he was three days without sight, and neither ate nor drank.* (Acts 9:8–9)

The Supernatural Fast

In a supernatural fast, an individual abstains from all solid foods and all liquids, including water. This fast occurs for a length of time that would normally be physically impossible to endure. Moses, Elijah, and Jesus each participated in this type of fast for forty consecutive days.

Our fasts, while they serve God, also serve us.

The books of Exodus, 1 Kings, and Matthew show examples of their supernatural fasts. The forty-day fasts of Moses, Elijah, and Jesus were supernatural fasts that occurred under supernatural conditions.

Moses

Moses' fast took place on Mount Sinai at a time when the leader of the twelve tribes of Israel was in the presence of the Almighty.

> *[27] Then the Lord said to Moses, "Write these words, for according to the tenor of these words I have made a covenant with you and with Israel."*

> *[28] So he was there with the Lord forty days and forty nights; he neither ate*

bread nor drank water. And He wrote on the tablets the words of the covenant, the Ten Commandments. (Exodus 34:27–28)

Elijah

Elijah's fast occurred under a far different set of circumstances. Queen Jezebel had ordered that the Old Testament prophet be put to death, and Elijah was running for his life. Afraid, weak, and weary, the prophet called on God to take his life; but God had far different plans for Elijah.

> *6 Then he looked, and there by his head was a cake baked on coals, and a jar of water. So he ate and drank, and lay down again.*
>
> *7 And the angel of the Lord came back the second time, and touched him, and said, "Arise and eat, because the journey is too great for you."*
>
> *8 So he arose, and ate and drank; and he went in the strength of that food forty days and forty nights as far as Horeb, the mountain of God.* (1 Kings 19:6–8)

Jesus

Jesus' forty-day fast is legendary. It happened in preparation for one of His most memorable trials—His testing in the desert. After fasting for forty days, Jesus resisted Satan's attempts to tempt Him.

> *¹ Then Jesus was led up by the Spirit into the wilderness to be tempted by the devil.*
>
> *² And when He had fasted forty days and forty nights, afterward He was hungry.*
> (Matthew 4:1–2)

The Normal Fast

In this type of fast, individuals abstain from all solid foods and liquids, with the exception of water. This fast is also known as a "pure fast." When you think of fasting today, a normal fast is most likely to be in your mind. It is the type of fast typically implemented by Christians in the modern world, and it is the type we will most often be discussing in this book.

What Is Not a Fast?

When discussing fasting, I have spoken to some people who believe that not wearing jewelry is a fast. The Bible clearly states in the book of Matthew that, when you fast, no one should know that you are fasting. Your countenance should remain the same as when you are not fasting.

Therefore, since fasting your jewelry changes your appearance, it cannot be considered a fast unto the Lord. Furthermore, there are no examples of abstaining from wearing jewelry as a fast in the Bible.

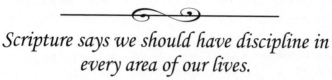

Scripture says we should have discipline in every area of our lives.

Some say that foregoing television is a fast. Again, there are no examples in the Bible to support this conclusion.

The Bible speaks of having discipline in every area of our lives.

> *And those who belong to Christ Jesus (the Messiah) have crucified the flesh (the godless human nature) with its passions and appetites and desires. If we live by the [Holy] Spirit, let us also walk by the Spirit. [If by the Holy Spirit we have our life in God, let us go forward walking in line, our conduct controlled by the Spirit.]* (Galatians 5:24–25 AMP)

You can say, "I am disciplining myself in the area of communication with God because I am no longer spending my afternoons glued to the television, watching soap operas. Instead, I will have a devotion and pray during this time." But, while this is a form of discipline, it is not a fast.

Fasting deals with abstaining from food and sometimes water. It is denying your physical body (or life) and crucifying your flesh to allow God's Spirit in you to be strengthened. The giving up of jewelry or television is a form of disciplining your flesh. There is a difference between disciplining your flesh and strengthening your spirit.

Fasting produces the kind of spiritual results that cause your spirit man to more readily surrender to God's will. It does this by weakening the natural man so that the spirit man can easily overcome him.

Use the tool of fasting. It will help you to see what God sees for your life. Your life will be effective for the purpose and destiny God has foreordained for you, for the kingdom, and for His glory. God can meet you, and use you, all the days of your life for the glory of His kingdom.

Let's review some spiritual benefits of fasting:

1. Empowers and strengthens your spirit man.

2. Enhances your prayer life.

3. Helps you to identify God's intervention in your life.

4. Helps you to focus on your Christian walk.

5. Helps you to identify the center of God's will for your life.

6. Disciplines your flesh.

Chapter Four

Preparing for a Fast

4

Preparing for a Fast

————•◦❧◦•————

*T*o succeed in a fast and reap all the benefits from it, you must prepare properly. Lack of preparation for a fast can lead to distractions, such as physical illness, which could cause you to fail in completing the fast.

In this section, I would like to introduce Professor Joe Carrington. He possesses a wealth of knowledge in the area of holistic medical nutrition that will serve as an asset for you. It is my hope that the knowledge gained in this chapter will further your purpose of bringing your heavenly Father glory in your physical body as well as in your spirit.

God's desire is for you to be victorious in every area of your life; Professor Carrington's knowledge of nutritional supplements could make the difference between achieving your goals during your fast or failing to complete it.

Professor Carrington is a senior fellow and institute professor at the New York Institute for Advanced Study, as well as a medical nutritionist, licensed by the Florida Board of Medicine. He holds various degrees, which include a master's degree in education from Harvard and graduate study in nuclear medicine at MIT (Massachusetts Institute of Technology).

Professor Carrington's contact information is included at the end of this book for your use. He has a heart to help all who cross his path, and he believes his office practice is also a ministry.

I know my meeting with Professor Carrington was not by chance; rather, it was a divine appointment for the purpose of sharing this valuable information with you. I asked him to write a chapter for this book, and he generously agreed to do so. The following is what he had to share.

The Medical Benefits of a Fast

Life is a miracle, and that means our bodies are miraculous creations of God! Our bodies are capable of the most amazing things, even when we don't take care of them as we should; but they can do even greater things when we do care for them.

Fasting is mentioned throughout the Bible, and in all references, it is used to strengthen one spiritually, as a sort of spiritual purification process. But fasting is also a physical purification process that has health benefits far beyond what anyone could have known in biblical days.

In this chapter, I am going to present two very important aspects of fasting: a concise description of the physical benefits of a fast and a method for increasing a fast's effectiveness by preparing beforehand.

The Physical Benefits of Fasting

When we fast, we eliminate food. The body no longer has an external source for the proteins, carbohydrates, sugars, and fats that it needs to perform its functions. Therefore, it begins to draw upon its reserves to supply what it needs to continue working.

There is about a three-day reserve of sugar (in the form of glycogen) stored in the liver and muscles to do this. But good things really begin to happen when these reserves run out. Once the body uses up its reserves, it then begins to draw upon other sources to supply what it needs. It begins to break down the tissues and cells to release the nutrients it requires. This is where the benefits of fasting really begin.

In our bodies, there are trillions of cells. Some of these cells are very healthy, but some of these cells are weak, malformed, and sick. These sick cells are the ones that get us into trouble and often cause cancer and other diseases.

When the body is deprived of food and begins to break down cells, it is the weak, sick cells that die first. Because they are weak, they cannot survive through a fast; they don't have the strength, so they are the first ones to die. This is a very good thing because, as they die off, the body is being cleansed and purged of those sick cells that may have developed into cancer and other diseases had they been left to do their damage. Since only the strong, healthy cells can survive through a fast, the body is left with only the very best, healthiest, and well-functioning cells at the end of a fast. Ridding the body of these sick cells could possibly save one's life by preventing numerous diseases.

In addition to the unhealthy cells dying off during a fast, the body also empties itself of the thousands of toxins that it is exposed to every day.

Often, it is these toxins that made those cells sick in the first place. They cause the cells to become mutagenic and evolve into cancers.

So, when the sick cells die, not only is the risk of developing cancers and illnesses reduced, but the toxins are also released and purged from the body. Nothing in modern medicine can do this! God built this miracle into the human body from the start and showed it to His children all throughout Scripture.

Since so many toxins and sick cells are literally dumped into the blood stream when one fasts, it is obvious that the body will have a lot to cope with. This brings us to the next section, which will deal with this situation and how to prepare for a fast.

Preparing for the Fast

Since the body will have to handle the toxins and dead, sick cells that will be released during a fast, it is only logical that one should prepare the body for the cleaning work it will need to do. The immune system is the key.

Before a fast, there are things that can be done to build up the immune system and make it strong so that it will be better suited to neutralize and dispose of the toxins and sick cells that will be released. This is a simple thing to do.

There are many elements to the immune system and each one does different things. The white blood cells, antibodies, natural killer cells, antioxidants etc., are all part of the arsenal that comprises the body's immune system. What a miracle the human body truly is!

There are nutritional supplements that one can take before a fast. These supplements will ready the immune system to handle the increased load of toxins and sick cells that will be released into the blood stream as one's body is being detoxified and cleansed during the fast. They are:

1. Vitamin C: I prefer Ester-C® since it is 400 percent better retained in the white blood cells after 24 hours than regular vitamin C, is pH neutral (won't irritate the stomach), and has less oxalic acid by-product, which means it is easier on the kidneys. Taking 2,000 milligrams three times daily is good for stimulating many aspects of the immune system.

2. Echinacea: This supplement is a well-known immune system stimulant that has the ability to increase immune

factors in the blood. It can be taken as directed on the bottle.

3. Multi-Max® (by KAL®) or Ultra-One® (by Nature's Plus®): These are multi-vitamin and mineral tablets that provide a decent amount of full spectrum nutrients, which are required for all aspects of immune system stimulation, in sustained release form. Take one tablet after breakfast.

4. MGN-3: This is a very special product that can increase natural killer cells (NK Cells) by as much as 300 percent. I use it in all my cancer protocols. Natural killer cells are extremely important and effective in searching out and destroying cells that are sick, mutated, likely to cause cancer, or already cancerous. NK cells are a natural part of the blood; they circulate throughout the body, searching for and destroying any cells that are sick before they can cause cancer or other troubles.

It takes about three months for NK cells to increase by 300 percent.

The dosage required is 1000 milligrams, three times daily for three months. Some people continue to take it after three months in lesser dosages, but it is expensive.

5. Antioxidants: All antioxidants, such as green tea, grape seed, vitamin E, resveratrol, sodium selenite (Twin Labs®), and vitamin A are beneficial in stimulating the immune system and preparing the body for a fast. Except for vitamin E, antioxidants can be taken as directed on the bottle's label. For vitamin E, follow Carrington's Rule: 1000 units natural vitamin E for every twenty years of age. Begin with 1000 units and increase by 1000 units every two weeks until the dose for your age is reached. In the case of high blood pressure, start at 400 units and then increase by 400 units every two weeks until your correct dose is reached.

In a perfect situation, this preparation can last three months because of the time needed for the MGN-3 to build up the NK cells. If one is in good health, one need not wait that long. If cancer is a concern, then the MGN-3 should be used during and after the fast. Please remember, this is information for a fast, not a full anti-cancer program.

When You Begin the Fast

Once the fast begins, one should discontinue all vitamins and nutrients. The reason for this is simple: Vitamins, nutrients, and antioxidants have a protective effect on *all* cells, including the sick ones. The purpose of the medical fast is to destroy and rid oneself of these sick cells, so we don't want to do anything to protect them. Taking nutrients during the fast would only protect these sick cells that we want to destroy. So once the fast begins, one should stop all nutrients except two: MGN-3 and potassium.

The MGN-3 will continue to promote the production of the NK cells that are needed to destroy sick and cancerous cells. Since it is not a nutrient or antioxidant, it will not protect the bad cells.

Also, one must take potassium. This is because the level of potassium in the blood drops during a fast. This will cause leg cramps and can be very dangerous since potassium is a key electrolyte for regulating heart rhythm. It also has a very narrow range—from 3.5–5.5 mEq/L (milli-equivalants per liter), with the desired value being 4.5 mEq/L. If one's potassium drops below 3.5, it becomes a serious danger to the heart and could precipitate an attack. Therefore, to avoid this and to have a safe, healthy fast, take one potassium tablet or capsule daily in the morning. Potassium pills will say "provides 99 milligrams of potassium" or "potassium...99 milligrams." Some say "potassium gluconate 590 milligrams" or "595 milligrams potassium gluconate (or citrate or aspartate). Each of these will yield 99 milligrams elemental potassium, which is what is needed.

During the Fast

During the fast, the only thing one should have is plain, pure water—nothing else (except the MGN-3 and potassium). This is because, as high levels of toxins are released into the blood, the detoxification mechanisms, particularly the kidneys, will be working very hard getting rid of all the undesirable materials.

They will need to be flushed clean continuously, and water is the way to do it. Remember, while things like green tea are good, they will provide antioxidants that can protect the bad cells and that is *not* desirable while one is fasting. So just drink plain, pure water and incorporate plenty of prayer. Eight ounces of pure water every hour is appropriate. Spend a few dollars and get one of those watches that beep every hour; let it remind you to have your water when it goes off.

Eight ounces is the amount of water the kidneys can clear every hour. Don't drink more because you will become waterlogged and feel uncomfortable.

Make sure you are drinking clean water. Water purified through reverse osmosis is the purest. Some companies provide a system that has a combination of reverse osmosis, charcoal, and deionization for the purest water on earth.

Mineral water is not desirable while fasting. It is already saturated with minerals and, during a fast, such saturation will decrease the water's ability to absorb and hold the toxins it needs to carry away. In other words, if the water has already absorbed minerals, it has little room to absorb anything else, and it cannot absorb the toxins.

After the Fast

After fasting, one should immediately reseed the intestine with good bacteria. There are many products providing acidophilus; I personally like to use those with a wide variety of good bacteria that also include the Bifidum type for the colon. During a fast, the normal intestinal bacteria can be altered, so reestablishing it with good bacteria is a good idea.

One should also begin by eating lightly, chewing food well, and having a variety of healthy foods.

The reason for the variety is to help promote and reestablish the intestinal flora (bacteria). Although there is much more to say on the subject of diet, nutrition, health, and disease, I am confining myself to a concise discussion of fasting for this book.

In His infinite wisdom, God made our bodies to be temples of His Holy Spirit. The body's ability to heal itself was placed in it by its divine Creator with miraculous abilities far beyond medical science. How much He must love us!

Chapter Five

Nine Biblical Examples of Fasting

5

Nine Biblical Examples of Fasting

———•⟨∞⟩•———

*W*hat follows are biblical examples of fasts. It is important to make sure that your fasting is scriptural by looking to Scripture for your direction. As you read, see how your own purposes fit with these examples of scriptural reasons for fasting.

To Gain Victory against the Enemy

This fast took place during a civil war between the tribe of Benjamin and other tribes of Israel. However, fasting can work against all enemies of God, including the opposing spiritual forces of the enemy.

> ²⁵ *And Benjamin went out against them from Gibeah on the second day, and cut down to the ground eighteen thousand more of the children of Israel; all these drew the sword.*
>
> ²⁶ *Then all the children of Israel, that is, all the people, went up and came to the house of God and wept. They sat there before the Lord and fasted that day until evening; and they offered burnt offerings and peace offerings before the Lord.*
> (Judges 20:25–26)

What resulted was a glorious Israelite victory over the Benjamites. (See verses 28–48.)

To Repent and Seek God's Mercy

Here are two examples of God's judgment, measured out to two kings: King Ahab and King David. The book of 2 Samuel speaks of David's sins when he saw the lovely Bathsheba, the wife of a loyal soldier in King David's army. Not only did King David covet another man's wife, lay with her, and conceive a child, but he also tried to cover it up, eventually sending Bathsheba's husband, Uriah, to the front lines of a fierce battle and commanding the soldiers around him to retreat, leaving him stranded with the enemy on all sides. Uriah was killed in the fighting. David's problems seemed to be over until the prophet Nathan visited him with news of God's punishment, which included the death of the child conceived by David and Bathsheba.

> *16 David therefore pleaded with God for the child, and David fasted and went in and lay all night on the ground.*
>
> *17 So the elders of his house arose and went to him, to raise him up from the ground. But he would not, nor did he eat food with them.* (2 Samuel 12:16–17)

Fasting didn't save the child's life. God was true to His word, but King David knew the value of faith and earnest fasting.

> *21 Then his servants said to him, "What is this that you have done? You fasted and wept for the child while he was alive, but when the child died, you arose and ate food."*
>
> *22 And he said, "While the child was alive, I fasted and wept; for I said, 'Who can tell whether the Lord will be gracious to me, that the child may live?'"*
>
> (2 Samuel 12:21–22)

King Ahab was also in trouble with God. His sins included following idols and killing Naboth over a piece of property. Ahab wanted Naboth's vineyard, but Naboth would not part with it. God had given the land to Naboth's father, and He told Naboth not to give up any of the inheritance from his father. Naboth obeyed God and refused to part with the vineyard. So Ahab had Naboth stoned to death. God used the prophet Elijah to tell Ahab of his sins and the resulting punishment.

> [27] *So it was, when Ahab heard those words, that he tore his clothes and put sackcloth on his body, and fasted and lay in sackcloth, and went about mourning.*
>
> [28] *And the word of the Lord came to Elijah the Tishbite, saying,*
>
> [29] *"See how Ahab has humbled himself before Me? Because he has humbled himself before Me, I will not bring the calamity in his days. In the days of his son I will bring the calamity on his house."*
>
> (1 Kings 21:27–29)

King Ahab wisely humbled himself with fasting, and that helped his cause. Though Ahab had sinned, God postponed His judgment against the king. Thank God for His mercy.

To Humble Ourselves before God

Ezra knew the importance of humility, even as he sought God's blessing of protection.

Then I proclaimed a fast there at the river of Ahava, that we might humble ourselves before our God, to seek from Him the right way for us and our little ones and all our possessions. (Ezra 8:21)

Ezra 8:31 records the result of their fasting:

Then we departed from the river of Ahava on the twelfth day of the first month, to go to Jerusalem. And the hand of our God was upon us, and He delivered us from the hand of the enemy and from ambush along the road.

To Ask God's Blessing and Help for a New Task

Esther was the queen of Persia, but that alone could not save her people, the Jews, from the threat of harsh treatment at the hands of her husband, King Ahasuerus. However, she took a bold stand and was victorious through fasting.

[15] Then Esther told them to reply to Mordecai:

[16] "Go, gather all the Jews who are present in Shushan, and fast for me; neither

eat nor drink for three days, night or day. My maids and I will fast likewise. And so I will go to the king, which is against the law; and if I perish, I perish!"
(Esther 4:15–16)

Esther did not perish. Her actions saved the people of Israel. (See Esther 7; 8:1–8.)

To Seek Revelation and Wisdom

Daniel, as the Old Testament shows, was a wise and learned man. He was smart enough to know that a man's knowledge is not the same as wisdom from God.

2 In the first year of his reign I Daniel understood by books the number of the years, whereof the word of the LORD came to Jeremiah the prophet, that he would accomplish seventy years in the desolations of Jerusalem.

3 And I set my face unto the Lord God, to seek by prayer and supplications, with fasting, and sackcloth, and ashes.
(Daniel 9:2–3 KJV)

Daniel's prayers, fueled by his fasting, worked.

Yea, whiles I was speaking in prayer, even the man Gabriel, whom I had seen in the vision at the beginning, being

94

caused to fly swiftly, touched me about the time of the evening oblation.

²² And he informed me, and talked with me, and said, O Daniel, I am now come forth to give thee skill and understanding. (Daniel 9:21–22 KJV)

To Mourn over Personal Sin and Failure

The people of Israel were made to see their sins through the prophet Joel. He called on God's people to seek the Lord's forgiveness and mourn their sin; this was necessary to prevent pestilence from devouring the land.

"Now, therefore," says the Lord, "Turn to Me with all your heart, with fasting, with weeping, and with mourning."
(Joel 2:12)

To Honor God

In the following verse, God told Zechariah to ask the priests and the prophets a very important question regarding the true purpose of fasting.

Ask all the people of the land and the priests, "When you fasted and mourned in the fifth and seventh months for the past seventy years, was it really for me that you fasted?" (Zechariah 7:5 NIV)

Fasting should only be done to honor God, not yourself.

> *Moreover, when you fast, do not be like the hypocrites, with a sad countenance. For they disfigure their faces that they may appear to men to be fasting. Assuredly, I say to you, they have their reward.*
> (Matthew 6:16)

Fasting should only be done to honor God, not yourself.

In the book of Luke, the Bible speaks of Anna, a prophetess. She is an example of a person who honors God.

> *And this woman was a widow of about eighty-four years, who did not depart from the temple, but served God with fastings and prayers night and day.* (Luke 2:37)

The fast you present to the Lord should always represent honor for God in servitude.

To Intercede on Behalf of Others

The book of Mark relates a time the disciples were unable to help a man because they had not prepared with the proper fasting and prayer. However, Jesus (who completed a forty-day fast) was able to rebuke the foul spirit that plagued the boy. This shows the importance of fasting when interceding for others.

> ²⁵ *When Jesus saw that the people came running together, He rebuked the unclean spirit, saying to it, "Deaf and dumb spirit, I command you, come out of him and enter him no more!"*
>
> ²⁶ *Then the spirit cried out, convulsed him greatly, and came out of him. And he became as one dead, so that many said, "He is dead."*
>
> ²⁷ *But Jesus took him by the hand and lifted him up, and he arose.*
>
> ²⁸ *And when He had come into the house, His disciples asked Him privately, "Why could we not cast it out?"*
>
> ²⁹ *So He said to them, "This kind can come out by nothing but prayer and fasting."* (Mark 9:25–29)

To Obtain a Commission from the Holy Spirit

The prophets and teachers in the church at Antioch sought the Lord with fasting and prayer.

> ² *As they ministered to the Lord, and fasted, the Holy Ghost said, Separate me*

> *Barnabas and Saul for the work where-*
> *unto I have called them.*
>
> *³ And when they had fasted and prayed,*
> *and laid their hands on them, they sent*
> *them away.* (Acts 13:2–3 KJV)

This resulted in the commission of Barnabas and Saul by the Holy Spirit to do the Lord's work on earth.

Chapter Six

Exposing the Spirit of Gluttony

6

Exposing the Spirit of Gluttony

———— •••◦◦◦••• ————

The first sin in the Bible, that of Adam and Eve, was over something as simple as food. This trend continues: There is a spirit of gluttony in the church today. This is evidenced by the fact that much of our fellowship and many of our celebrations are centered around incredible amounts of food. This spirit has plagued the church long enough.

In the same manner that we acknowledge discipline in abstaining from sin, we must also acknowledge any lack of discipline in our eating habits. The Bible is very clear on the subject of having discipline in every area of our lives.

Satan loves to cause the opposite of truth by distorting the appearance of truth.

Satan has given the spirit of gluttony the assignment of infiltrating the church. He loves to cause the opposite of truth by distorting the appearance of truth. I was prompted by the Holy Spirit to include this chapter to expose Satan's plan to destroy our temples (bodies) through the spirit of gluttony.

The Robe of Righteousness

The Bible says we should walk in the light with discipline in all areas of our lives.

> *I say then: Walk in the Spirit, and you shall not fulfill the lust of the flesh.*
> (Galatians 5:16)

We must glorify the Father in our minds, in our bodies, and in our spirits. Mind, spirit, and body. We, as the church, need to recognize the importance of our physical bodies. We are the temples, and our bodies are the vessels that God uses to "house" His glory. We are to keep our vessels, His tabernacles, disciplined in all areas so that He can manifest His power through anointing, for the working of signs, wonders, and miracles.

We accomplish this by exercising repentance in our lives. Repentance is the beginning of righteousness. The moment you accepted Jesus Christ as your Savior and asked Him into your heart, you were covered by Jesus' righteousness.

After we accept His gift of salvation, He bestows His robe of righteousness upon each one of us forever. From that moment forward, we are given a fresh start as born-again believers.

> *Namely, the righteousness of God which comes by believing with personal trust and confident reliance on Jesus Christ (the Messiah). [And it is meant] for all who believe. For there is no distinction.*
> (Romans 3:22 AMP)

Can you envision Him placing His robe of righteousness upon you?

I had a vision concerning this. I saw a man walking down a street with his head bowed over in a slumped position, dragging part of his coat behind him. It was cold and rainy outside, and he was struggling to get to where he was going. He was wearing a coat, but only one of his arms was through the coat's sleeve. The other arm, and part of his body, was exposed and vulnerable to the brutal weather. In this state, he was not a portrait of a man walking in victory but of a man walking in defeat. All at once, he took notice of his coat's protective benefits and promptly asked his Father to readjust it for him. His Father responded immediately and put it on correctly by putting both of His son's arms through the coat sleeves and buttoning it.

I believe the same is true of the robe of righteousness and the gift of repentance. When we become careless and forget to keep the robe of Christ's righteousness on properly, we suffer the consequences. However, it is when we take notice of the robe's value, come to our Father in repentance, and allow Him to readjust the robe of His righteousness for us that we triumph over the elements that plague us.

We are made righteous by His covering—a covering that embraces us from the inside out, causing us to live successful lives. His robe of righteousness is a defensive weapon that protects us from the enemy! It is ours for eternity. It never loses its effectiveness against the enemy. However, if we do not know how to wear it correctly, it is of little value, for its effectiveness in protecting us is predicated on how we choose to wear it. Too many of us are walking around with His robe

unbuttoned, unfastened, or only partially covering us.

---

*We are made righteous by His covering—
a covering that embraces us from
the inside out.*

Satan loves it when we allow ourselves to get
complacent about wearing our robes. But God is
aware of how we choose to wear His righteousness
and, through His Spirit, endeavors to show us when
our robes are not being worn correctly. It is the
prompting of the Holy Spirit that will reveal a different way to do something—a way contrary to the
course of action we may have previously decided
on—simply to promote a good witness of who God is
in our lives. In this way, the Spirit's prompting con-
victs us and bring us to repentance, causing God to
be exalted by the victories He blesses us with. It is
our responsibility to use this tool of repentance.

> *And having been set free from sin, you
> have become the servants of righteous-
> ness (of conformity to the divine will in
> thought, purpose, and action).*
> (Romans 6:18 AMP)

Repentance is the only vehicle that allows God
to readjust the robe to its rightful place, bringing
us to live lives of triumph instead of defeat.

We must take charge of the maintenance of our temples, through repentance, for the express purpose of using our bodies as appropriate "filters" for God's glory to manifest itself—for the benefit of signs, wonders, and miracles that draw others to the salvation knowledge of who God is. If we carelessly allow our filters to become clogged with unwanted particles of dirt (sin), we will eventually become ill-equipped to handle the flow of His glory in an unhindered manner.

He uses us as instruments for His glory. He sends His glory out to operate in and through us at the appointed time, in conjunction with our spiritual gifts, to bring a harvest of souls into His kingdom. Then He receives His glory back, with the added bonus of the recognition due to Him for who He is and what He has accomplished through us.

If we are to bring God glory through the victories in our lives, we must be aware of the spirit of gluttony. We must examine ourselves and expose this vile spirit.

We must expose this demon's crafty delusion, which causes us to crave food as a form of satisfaction. The Bible tells us that we, as Christians, have the authority of Christ, given to us by Him, to control the demonic forces that try to oppress us. We have the authority to bind them and render them inoperative in our lives.

> *And I will give unto thee the keys of the kingdom of heaven: and whatsoever thou shalt bind on earth shall be bound in heaven: and whatsoever thou shalt loose on earth shall be loosed in heaven.*
> (Mathew 16:19 KJV)

Take the authority you have in Christ and command the spirit of gluttony to cease operating in your life. The spirit of gluttony, if you are not careful, will try to exalt itself as a god in your life. Render this spirit inoperative in the name of Jesus. You have the authority through Christ!

Bring your body into subjection to who God is. Too often, we find ourselves, as a church, witnessing to the lost about the victories we have in Jesus. And yet many of us across this nation—pastors included—are victims of the spirit of gluttony. The world sees us living our lives with lack of discipline and control in the area of eating. We struggle with the battle of overeating.

Today, the appearance of the church in the area of overeating has caused us to become false testimonies of victory in this area of our lives.

Why? We show ourselves as poor examples in this area; and we do not bring glory to God. We speak of discipline, of victory in all areas, but our appearance declares a different testimony. Unfortunately, overeating is a testimony of failure and defeat.

Satan's main objective is to "steal, kill, and destroy."

> *The thief cometh not, but for to steal, and to kill, and to destroy: I am come that they might have life, and that they might have it more abundantly.* (John 10:10 KJV)

Our bodies are temples of the Holy Spirit, which God uses to house His glory. Our bodies, by themselves, should declare to the world: "I am subjected to the will of the Father because of my desire for victory in and through my life as a Christian, and, as an ambassador to the Most High, being disciplined in every area of my life."

Chapter Seven

Presenting Your Fast as unto the Lord

7

Presenting Your Fast as unto the Lord

———•—•—◄❀►—•—•———

*T*he book of Isaiah, chapter 58, offers the best instruction in presenting your fast as unto the Lord, as well as the best description of the subsequent benefits of your fast.

As I mentioned earlier, I incorporated fasting into my walk last year. I began fasting one meal a week, which led to my fasting one meal every other day.

One evening, while in prayer, the Lord said to my spirit, "I require a pure fast (a normal fast)." I was willing to do what the Lord asked, but I did not understand what a pure fast meant. So I asked in prayer, "Father, show me what you mean." I felt led to open the Bible and God brought me to the book of Isaiah, chapter 58. There, I discovered the answers to all my questions.

Based on the book of Isaiah, you should present your fast as unto the Lord in the following manner:

1. You should not spend the day (or days) of your fast in the same way you spend the days you do not fast. You must endeavor to labor in the spirit rather than in the natural.

    Why have we fasted, they say, and You do not see it? Why have we afflicted ourselves, and You take no knowledge [of it]? Behold [O Israel], on the day of your fast [when you should be grieving for your sins], you find profit in your business, and [instead of stopping all work, as the law implies you and your workmen should do] you extort from your hired servants a full amount of labor.
    (Isaiah 58:3 AMP)

    How do you labor in the spirit? You labor in the spirit through praise, worship, and interceding for others in prayer.

2. God has no time, or patience, to hear any fasting for strife or debate.

[The facts are that] you fast only for strife and debate and to smite with the fist of wickedness. Fasting as you do today will not cause your voice to be heard on high.
(Isaiah 58:4 AMP)

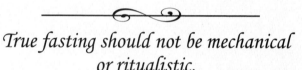

True fasting should not be mechanical or ritualistic.

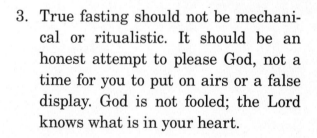

3. True fasting should not be mechanical or ritualistic. It should be an honest attempt to please God, not a time for you to put on airs or a false display. God is not fooled; the Lord knows what is in your heart.

Is such a fast as yours what I have chosen, a day for a man to humble himself with sorrow in his soul? [Is true fasting merely mechanical?] Is it only to bow down his head like a bulrush and to spread sackcloth and ashes under him [to indicate a condition of heart that

he does not have]? Will you call this a
fast and an acceptable day to the Lord?
(Isaiah 58:5 AMP)

Practical Steps for Your Fast

In reveiw, here are some steps that will improve the spiritual impact of your fast.

Be sure to prepare your body for a fast. Why? God wants us to triumph in all our ways, and preparation ensures a successful and healthy fast.

As much as possible, put aside all the things of this world, letting your focus rest on God. You can use the time you would usually spend preparing and eating food to seek God. Find a quiet place with no distractions and spend some quality time with your Savior.

Try to be in a position of worship throughout the day and make sure you pray often during this important time in your Christian walk.

Jesus' Example of Fasting

Jesus fasted for forty days. The Bible tells us that He went up into the wilderness. He, too, separated Himself from the distractions of this world.

The Savior's forty-day fast prepared His natural man for the world's temptations. He practiced His future death on the cross through the crucifying of His natural flesh; and by that same death of natural flesh, He withstood the temptations of Satan. He crucified the flesh and overcame the natural man not once, but twice: once in the desert and once on the cross. How? Through fasting!

Fasting gave Him the needed ammunition to fight against His natural, human will and to allow the will of the Father to be done instead.

Jesus drew strength from His period of fasting, which propelled Him to the next level: victory at the cross!

Exercising Your Spirit Man

There is always a price to be paid for the results you seek. In weight training, or training for any kind of physical event, you must condition your body.

Similarly, to condition your spirit, you should exercise the tool of fasting in your life. Although fasting should be coupled with prayer, it should also be considered a separate spiritual exercise. It is not a mere supplement to prayer; it is a form of worship in itself. Fasting can be seen as prayer without words, keeping your thoughts in communication with God, instead of with desires of the flesh.

Perhaps God has put in your spirit a task to accomplish. Through the use of fasting and prayer in your life, you can stay focused. You can fulfill your purpose and destiny. Remember, He knew you even before you were conceived in your mother's womb.

> *Before I formed you in the womb I knew [and] approved of you [as My chosen instrument], and before you were born I separated and set you apart, consecrating you; [and] I appointed you as a prophet to the nations.*
>
> (Jeremiah 1:5 AMP)

God had a purpose and destiny for your life before you were born.

Fasting can be seen as prayer without words, keeping your thoughts in communication with God.

Do you want His purpose and destiny to come to fruition sooner in your life? Then give His Spirit the strength to overcome. You can strengthen your spirit man through repentance, praise, worship, prayer, and fasting.

Fasting will give His purpose and destiny the added strength to develop into a reality in your life.

In submission to God, I fasted for a year and six months, eating only one meal a day. During that time, God revealed the need for me to share this information with you. I believe that God wanted to bring me to a higher level in my walk. I believe that He wants to accomplish the specific task—for which this fasting will serve as a weapon of strength against the enemy's distractions—of keeping me focused on the path He has called me to.

God has created us differently—as individuals. I believe that if you are sensitive to the Holy Spirit, He will help you reach the center of God's will for your life. He will give you the power to improve your Christian walk by increasing your desire for prayer, or praise and worship, or fasting, or by increasing your desire to read His Word. God will bring you to a greater level of intimacy with Himself.

In all of these ways—prayer, fasting, worship, reading His Word—God can direct you to walk in the way that best serves Him at that present time, in the way that will cause victory in your life through the accomplishment of the task. The purpose and destiny God has put into your heart can become a reality.

The Lord will guide you continually.

And the Lord shall guide you continually and satisfy you in drought and in dry places and make strong your bones. And you shall be like a watered garden and like a spring of water whose waters fail not. (Isaiah 58:11 AMP)

Delight yourself in the Lord and He will make you ride on the high places of the earth.

Then will you delight yourself in the Lord, and I will make you to ride on the high places of the earth, and I will feed you with the heritage [promised for you] of Jacob your father; for the mouth of the Lord has spoken it.
(Isaiah 58:14 AMP)

God wants to reveal to us more of who He is. We know of His benefits; now let's get to know Him better.

Fasting is a wonderful tool in building your relationship with God, Jesus, and the Holy Spirit. Try fasting; it will change your life!

I choose to end this book with a quotation from Franklin Hall.

> The truth of fasting is being revealed to us now that we may secure the greater things of God, that we may receive the "gifts of the Spirit," and that a mighty worldwide revival of spiritual power will sweep over the world, with major signs and miracles in these last days.[3]

Honor, glory and praise be to our heavenly Father, forever and ever!

---

[3] Reverend F. Hall, *Atomic Power with God with Fasting and Prayer*, page 9.

Notes of Appreciation

For the words of this book and for making it possible for them to be shared with others, I first and foremost thank God, the Holy Spirit, and Jesus our Savior.

I would like to thank the following people, who contributed to the book, whether in testimony, prayer, fasting, or wonderful encouragement.

Thank you, Pastor Lloyd Bustard, for writing the forward for this book.

Thank you, Professor Carrington, CAS., N.C., MED., for your contribution to this project.

Thank you, Drs. Ken and Mary Jane Brewer, for the inclusion of your testimony in this book.

Thank you, Pastors Meredith and San Singletary, for the addition of your testmony to this project.

Thank you, Associate Pastor Richard H. Meisel, for your contribution to this project.

Thank you, Sister Bernadette Clayborne, for sharing your testimony.

Special thanks to Melba Lugo and Mariana for their continued support and prayers, offered on behalf of this project.

Thank you to Doug Lyons for your patience and help with this book.

Thank you, Kaitlin Domanoski. I appreciate your enthusiasm, punctual approach, candid and insightful remarks, and your patience with the editing of this project. I have enjoyed working with you!

Thank you, Pastor Antoinette Cericola, for being my "Teach" and supporting me in all my endeavors.

Thank you to my supportive and loving sister Sally and her family. I love you!

To Mom and Dad, Norma and Elvin Fuster. Although you are in heaven, I wanted you to know that I will always love you and I'll see you up there one day.

I also dedicate this book to Robbie—my God-sent son.

Special thanks to Grandma and Grandpa, Gail and Bob, who never said "no" when asked to watch the children as I embarked on this venture. Love you both!

A big thank you to all those who I may not have mentioned by name, but who, with their prayers, love, and encouragement, helped make this project a reality.

Special Notes

Professor Joe Carrington

Office address:
8184 Wiles Road
Coral Springs, FL 33067
Phone: (954) 344–1604

Services: Full-practice holistic medical nutrition-ist. Prevention and treatment of all medical conditions and diseases (physical and mental), including, but not limited to: cardiology, gerontology, neurology, internal psychiatry and psychology, immunology, life extension, and preventative nutrition.

Founder of Harvard Research Associates, the creators of Smart Baby—the world's first pre-natal vitamin designed to raise a baby's IQ by improving brain development. For use in pregnant and breast-feeding women around the world.
Visit: www.smartbaby.net

Dr. Carrington can be heard on Mondays 11:00 a.m. to 1:00 p.m., on WAXY 790 AM, broadcast out of South Florida.

Drs. Ken and Mary Jane Brewer

Presidents and founders of Brewer Christian College and Graduate School in Jacksonville, Florida. To learn more about the undergraduate and graduate programs now available, visit: www.brewerchristiancollege.com.

Dr. Mary Jane Brewer is also the founder and director of Women's International Network, "networking women together for the purposes of God." Visit: www.winforchrist.com

Pastor Lloyd Bustard

Founder of World Worship Center, Charlotte, North Carolina

E-mail: worldworshipcenter@yahoo.com
        info@lloydbustard.com

For an itinerary or information about the ministry, visit: www.lloydbustard.com.

Associate Pastor Richard Meisel

President of Hall Deliverance Foundation, Phoenix, Arizona.

To order a catalog of written works on fasting, faith, and full baptism with Holy Spirit fire, contact:

Hall Deliverance Foundation, Inc.
Box 9910
Phoenix, AZ 85068
Phone: (602) 944–5711

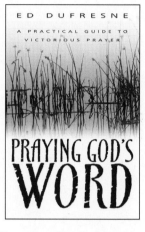

ANOTHER POWERFUL BOOK
from Whitaker House

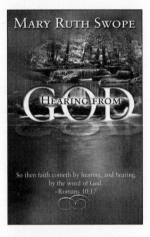

Hearing from God
Mary Ruth Swope

God wants to speak to you personally every day. He is
calling you, and He wants you to hear Him. Do you know
His voice? Mary Ruth Swope reveals how you can hear
from God and receive divine guidance for every aspect of
your life. Once you have begun to recognize His voice,
you'll know that He is with you, giving you power for every
step you take.

ISBN: 0-88368-663-5 • Trade • 224 pages

Warsaw &
Gdańsk

CONTENTS